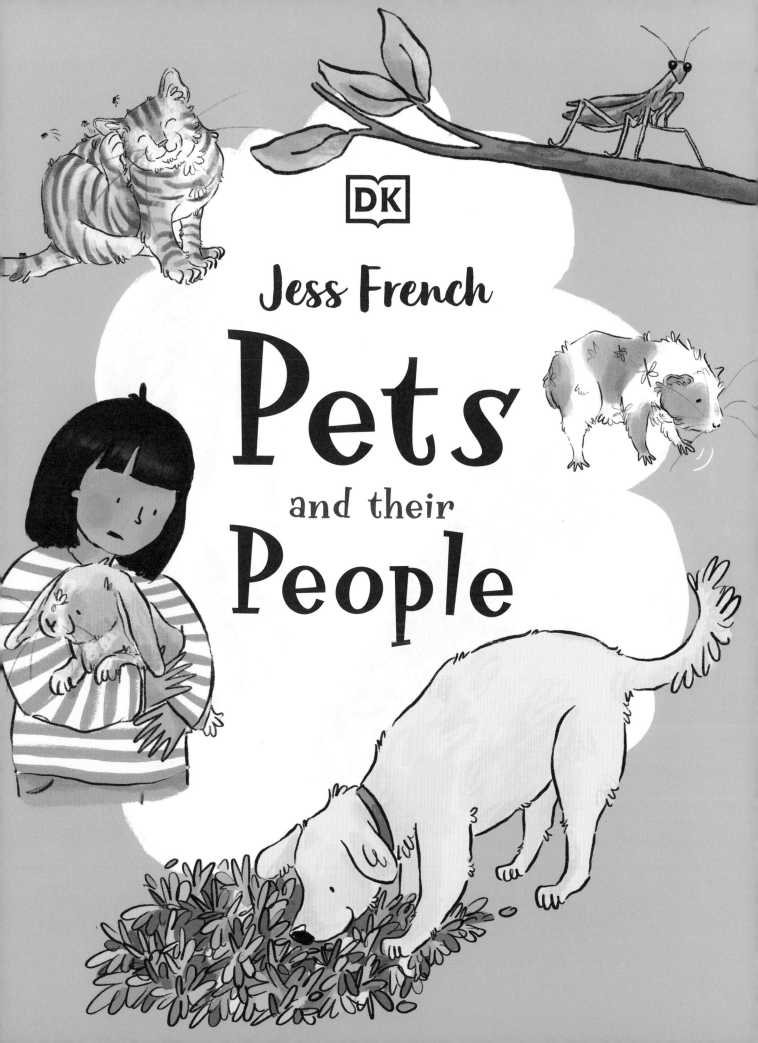

DK

Jess French

Pets
and their
People

DK | Penguin Random House

Author Jess French
Illustrator Becca Hall
Project Editor Sophie Parkes
Senior Art Editor Rachael Parfitt Hunt
Editor Sarah MacLeod
Designers Sif Nørskov, Hannah Moore, Karen Hood
Jacket Designer Rachael Parfitt Hunt
Production Editor Abi Maxwell
Production Controller Francesca Sturiale
Jacket Coordinator Magda Pszuk
Managing Editor Penny Smith
Deputy Art Director Mabel Chan
Publisher Sarah Larter

First published in Great Britain in 2023 by
Dorling Kindersley Limited
DK, One Embassy Gardens, 8 Viaduct Gardens,
London, SW11 7BW

The authorised representative in the EEA is
Dorling Kindersley Verlag GmbH. Arnulfstr. 124,
80636 Munich, Germany

Text copyright © Dr Jess French 2023
Illustration copyright © Becca Hall 2023
Layout and design copyright © 2023 Dorling Kindersley Limited
A Penguin Random House Company
10 9 8 7 6 5 4 3 2
001–332941–Apr/2023

A CIP catalogue record for this book
is available from the British Library.
ISBN: 978-0-2415-8508-5

Printed and bound in China

For the curious
www.dk.com

MIX
Paper | Supporting
responsible forestry
FSC™ C018179

This book was made with Forest Stewardship
Council™ certified paper – one small step in
DK's commitment to a sustainable future.

For more information go to
www.dk.com/our-green-pledge

Contents

JESS'S TIP

Throughout this book, keep your eyes peeled for my tip sections, where I offer helpful facts and advice to help you with any pets or animals!

Spot me and my friends throughout the book!

Hello!

I'm Jess - I'm an author and vet, and my life has been shaped by animals. From the moment I was born, I slept next to a ginger cat called Claws, and for 13 years she was by my side. She gave me great joy and comfort. When I was four, I had a bassett hound dog called Monty. His kennel was my refuge when I was sad, and his warm body and slobbery licks never failed to cheer me up.

I'm lucky to have led a life filled with animal friends. I don't like to say that I have "owned" many pets, for I feel they owned me as much as I did them. But I have loved many animals - dogs, cats, rabbits, gerbils, lizards, praying mantises, snakes… All of them have made me the person I am today. And I know that all over the world, other people are loving animals in just the same way.

I have written this book as a celebration of that love. It's a book for those who have pets, those who don't, those who would like a pet, and those who like to appreciate animals from afar. It is the first book I have written without my beloved cat, Taffy, sitting on my shoulder as I type. I miss her every day but I am also very grateful for the times we shared and I know my life was better for having had her in it. So this one's for you, Taffy. And for anyone who has ever loved an animal friend.

With love,

Jess French

Jess French

History of pets

A very long time ago, all animals were wild - there were no pets! Over many years, people tamed wild animals to use them for food, to work them, and to keep them as companions. This process is called domestication.

I was probably the first ever pet!

I can carry heavy loads for humans.

Dogs
Modern dogs are related to wild wolves. They probably started helping us with hunting and living with us as pets more than 16,000 years ago, in Asia.

Pigs and cattle
Humans probably started taming pigs and cows around 8000 BCE. They were found across Asia, Europe, and the Middle East. Each area usually preferred to keep either pigs or cows.

AROUND **30000** BCE ▶ AROUND **9000** BCE ▶ AROUND **8000** BCE ▶ AROUND **5500** BC

Chickens, sheep, and goats
About 11,000 years ago, humans probably kept chickens for meat and eggs, whilst sheep and goats provided meat, milk, and wool.

Donkeys and guinea pigs
Archaeologists think that donkeys were first used by humans to carry heavy loads through deserts. Around the same time, people living in the Andes mountains in South America were probably the first to domesticate guinea pigs for food.

PETS OF THE PAST

Although most of these animals were used for work or food, their domestication paved the way for pets as we know them today! Many of our domestic animals look very different to their wild ancestors.

Reindeer
New evidence suggests that reindeer were domesticated by humans in the Arctic as recently as 2,000 years ago. We think they were used to pull sleds across the snow.

Camels
Archaeologists believe that camels were used to transport heavy goods such as copper across the Middle East.

Oxen, llamas, and honey bees
Oxen were possibly used to pull sledges or ploughs. Llamas were first kept in the Andes mountains for their wool, meat, dung, and hides. Humans started to keep honey bees in artificial homes, called hives.

AROUND **4000** BCE   AROUND **2500** BCE   AROUND **1000** BCE   AROUND **100** BCE

Ducks
Ducks were probably kept by humans in Southeast Asia for their meat and eggs.

Dogs

Humans and dogs have lived together for thousands of years. At first, they were attracted to our camps by warm fires and food scraps. Now, a third of human families share their home with a dog.

Super smell

Dogs can sniff out things that are very far away. They can even use each of their nostrils independently to smell different things!

Woof!

We are brilliant at letting you know how we feel. As well as using our body language, we can whine, growl, howl, and bark.

Sharp teeth are perfect for biting, tearing, and crunching different types of food.

DOG FAMILY

Domestic dogs are part of an animal family called "canids", which includes wild animals such as coyotes, foxes, wolves, dingoes, and jackals.

Coyote

Fox

Wolf

Dingo

Jackal

Different shapes and sizes

All domestic dogs looked quite similar until humans started to breed them together in particular ways to create the dogs we have today. Now dogs come in many shapes and sizes.

It is humans' responsibility to breed dogs in a way that means they can have happy, healthy lives.

Poodle

Labrador

Labradoodle

+ =

Dogs are very intelligent. They can be trained to follow all sorts of different commands.

Walkies!

For many people, sharing a daily walk is one of the best bits about caring for a dog. Doing this exercise every day has lots of health benefits for both humans and dogs.

In many countries, it is the law for a dog to wear a collar with its family's details on it, so the dog can be returned if it gets lost.

DOGS NEED AT LEAST ONE WALK EVERY DAY.

9

Cats

Cats are incredible hunters. They first became part of human life thousands of years ago, when they were used to catch mice that would scurry around our grain stores. These days, cats are more likely to be found lounging on our sofas or chasing our shoelaces.

A mummified cat ......

HISTORY

Throughout history, cats have been both honoured and feared. In Ancient Egypt, cats were mummified, worshipped, and treated like royalty. In other places, people believed that cats belonged to witches and were actually the devil in disguise!

My eyes can reflect light, which helps me to see when it is dark.

Excellent eyesight

A cat's pupils can tell you how it is feeling. When it's relaxed, its pupils are shaped like slits. But when it's excited or shocked, they become large and round.

Cats tuck their claws away when they are not in use, keeping them sharp.

Protractile claws

Sharp teeth ······

Built to climb
Cats feel safer above ground. Their strong legs and sharp claws make them excellent climbers.

JESS'S TIP

Each cat in your house should have its own quiet place to go to the toilet, away from its food and water.

Hunters

Cats are meat eaters. Their sharp teeth and claws are perfect for catching and killing their prey, and their spiky tongues help them to scrape meat from bones.

Loners
Cats usually prefer to be alone than to spend time with other cats.

Scratching post and ropes

Grooming

Cats spend as much as half their day keeping clean! They wipe their faces with their paws and comb their fur with their tongues.

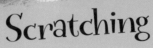

Scratching

Cats scratch for three reasons; to stretch out their legs, to keep their claws sharp, and to mark their territories. Teaching your cat to use a scratching post will save your furniture from a lot of damage!

11

Guinea pigs

There's never a quiet moment if you have guinea pigs in your family! These chatty little creatures love to explore and are happiest in big groups - they can often be heard squeaking at one another to stay in touch.

We're friendly guinea pigs! We're also sometimes known as cavies.

Furry friends

In the wild, guinea pigs love hanging out with their friends. They are usually found in groups of up to 20 individuals, so it is really important that you never keep just one guinea pig alone. Also, while guinea pigs love to live with other guinea pig friends, it's not a good idea to let them live with rabbits, who can hurt them and give them nasty diseases.

GUINEA PIG HISTORY

Guinea pigs haven't always been kept as pets. The first captive guinea pigs were kept to be eaten, rather than to become part of the family.

Making your guinea pig feel at home

Guinea pigs need a large hutch to shelter in when the weather is bad, and plenty of tunnels and pipes where they can hide. They will also need a large run, where they can spend their days happily munching on grass.

Make sure your guinea pig lives with other guinea pigs to keep it happy and healthy.

If your guinea pig hutch is outside, keep it out of the wind in a sheltered place.

Guinea pigs love to gnaw on wood! Giving them something to chew keeps their teeth and brains happy.

In the wild, guinea pigs are prey animals, who think that any bigger animal coming near them wants to eat them, so picking guinea pigs up might be scary for them. Get to know your guinea pig slowly. They will soon give you signs if they are happy to be snuggled and stroked!

Vitamin guinea

Humans and guinea pigs have something in common - neither of them can make their own vitamin C! Vitamin C is really important to keep guinea pigs (and people!) healthy, so make sure you buy good quality food specially made for guinea pigs and containing vitamin C.

WHAT'S ON THE MENU?

Most of their diet should be grass and hay, with a sprinkling of guinea pig pellets and a few fresh fruits and vegetables.

Hay

Bell peppers

Carrot tops

Celery

Guinea pig pellets

Fish

They may not be soft and cuddly, but fish are quiet and fascinating to watch. It's no surprise that they have been kept as pets for thousands of years!

SOMETHING FISHY

There are two main types of fish kept as pets – freshwater fish and marine fish. They live in totally different conditions and should never be kept in the same tank.

History
Goldfish were first bred in China more than 4,500 years ago. In the 18th century, they were brought to England and have been kept as pets ever since.

Freshwater fish

Freshwater fish come from rivers, lakes, ponds and streams. They live in water that is low in salt, so pet freshwater fish must have a tank filled with the right kind.

Tanks should always look clean, with no algae or build-up of food.

Plants provide places for fish to hide when they are scared.

Looking after your fish

What kind of water does your fish need? Saltwater or freshwater? Warm or cold? Once you know what kind of tank you are going to create, you will also need to think about these things:

How will you make sure the water stays at the right temperature?

What kind of filter will you use to keep the water clean?

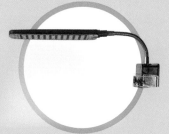

How will you give your fish the right amount of light?

JESS'S TIP!

Goldfish bowls are never appropriate for keeping fish in, as they are far too small. Fish tanks should always be as big as possible and be kept away from direct sunlight and loud noises.

Marine fish

Marine fish are bright, mesmerising, and beautiful. In the wild, they are found in the ocean.

Marine fish live in water that is salty. We cannot survive in water from taps.

BUBBLE! BUBBLE!

You can decorate our tank with ornaments and gravel.

Small furries

Cute, fluffy, and fascinating to watch, little mammals are firm favourites with families around the world. While many of the different species look quite similar, the space and attention they need can vary, so do your research before choosing who to welcome into your home.

Gerbil

These busybodies love to burrow and dig, and they are constantly on the move. This makes gerbils fun to watch, but not so great to cuddle.

Chinchilla

Soft and silky chinchillas were originally bred by humans for their fur. They are very shy and like to be in the company of other chinchillas. They are also are very active, so they need a lot of space.

I can be a little stinky, but you'll get used to it!

Ferret

Playful and curious ferrets can be trained to do all kinds of tricks, but they need their human companion to spend plenty of time with them to keep them out of mischief.

Small furries can be easily frightened by larger animals such as cats and dogs. If you have other pets at home, keep your small furries in a separate area of the house, where they will feel safer.

Rat

Rats are playful and very smart. They learn quickly and make strong bonds with their human companions. To prevent them from getting bored and to make sure they get enough exercise, rats need to come out and play for at least an hour each day.

RODENTS

Many small, furry pets belong to a family of mammals called "rodents". There are around 1,500 different species and they are found all over the planet. Rodents have sharp front teeth that are constantly growing.

Mouse

Mice would prefer to spend time with each other rather than humans, so they make better pets if you are interested in watching rather than cuddling.

Hamster

Cute, fluffy hamsters are very common pets. They are famous for their stretchy cheek pouches, which they use for storing food. Millions of hamsters live in human homes all around the world.

Degu

Degus are very sociable creatures, and love to have lots of other other degus to cosy up with. They are very active and require a lot of space with plenty of toys to keep them occupied.

Sleepy hamster

Don't worry if I seem to spend the whole day sleeping. I'm nocturnal, which means I'm most active at night.

Rabbits

While they are known for being brilliant jumpers, rabbits are also expert burrowing animals. They love to dig and find soft, cosy spots to sleep.

Large ears listen out for danger

Rabbits feel safest together in big groups.

Alien invaders

There are millions of rabbits all over the world. In many places, they were first introduced by humans, who brought them as food. However, rabbits breed very quickly and their numbers can rapidly increase, so in many countries they are now considered pests.

I am built for grazing on grass. To make sure my teeth don't get ground away by my constant chomping, they never stop growing!

Thumper

Rabbits use their strong back legs to quickly hop or run from predators. They also thump the ground when they are frightened.

Front paws are used for burrowing

Super sleepers

Rabbits are crepuscular, which means they are most active at dawn and dusk. It's very normal for them to spend the whole day resting or sleeping.

.... A binky hop

Happy bunnies

When rabbits are really happy or excited they do a special movement called a binky hop, where they jump and twist their bodies. Give your rabbit plenty of space, so it can binky hop as much as it likes!

Under the ground

Wild rabbits make their homes underground in warrens. These are huge networks of tunnels with many entrance and exit holes, which allow the rabbits to escape from predators. Warrens also contain larger chambers where rabbits make their nests and leave their young. Try to recreate this environment when making a home for your rabbit - a hutch alone is not enough.

EATING POO

Grass is hard for the body to break down, so rabbits eat it twice! They produce soft poos called caecotrophs, which they eat directly from their bottoms, giving them a second chance to absorb the nutrients.

Digging is an important part of a rabbit's life. If you don't allow a rabbit to dig, it can become very stressed.

19

Tortoises and turtles

Tortoises and turtles have been kept as pets for hundreds of years. They are fascinating creatures that live for a very long time, but they have complex needs, so they can be tricky pets to keep.

Tortoises

Tortoises are well-adapted to life on land. Sturdy legs help them lug around heavy shells.

The shell

Tortoises and turtles have hard, bony shells for protection. Many tortoises can pull their heads and legs into their shells to keep themselves safe from attack. Shells also help to keep them warm, as they can absorb heat from the Sun.

TORTOISES AS PETS

Tortoises have been around for millions of years and are found all over the world. When they were first kept as pets, they were taken from the wild. Now, this is not allowed – tortoises sold as pets must be bred in captivity.

Eating and drinking

Most tortoises are herbivores and spend most of the day chomping on plants. Each species has a slightly different diet, so find out which plants provide the nutrients your tortoise needs. Tortoises also need access to fresh water – they will often climb right into their bowls before dipping their heads to drink!

I love to roam, so give me plenty of space to explore!

Pool of drinking water

Escape artists

Tortoises love to explore. Although they move slowly, they have extremely strong legs, which makes them excellent escape artists. Beware when making your garden escape-proof: tortoises can push boulders and bricks out of the way.

Keeping your tortoise

In the past, tortoises have mostly been kept in gardens. But for most tortoises to grow and be healthy, they need a little more specialist care.

JESS'S TIP

A tortoise can live for up to 150 years, so if you get one as a pet, it could outlive you!

Tortoises need lots of space, so a cage won't do. They need sunshine and fresh air, but mustn't get too cold, so they often need both an indoor and outdoor area.

To survive winter, some tortoises spend the colder months sleeping, which is known as hibernation. It is important to learn about this process so you can help your tortoise to hibernate safely.

To keep your tortoise healthy, it's important to keep it at the right temperature and to make sure it gets enough sunlight.

150

Turtles

Unlike tortoises, turtles spend a lot of time in the water. Most pet turtles are from freshwater environments, and have webbed feet and flattened bodies to help them travel easily through rivers and ponds.

Terrapins need a tank with water and an area for basking.

Greenery

Terrapins

There are more than 126 terrapin species worldwide. The red-eared terrapin is most commonly kept as a pet. Like tortoises, terrapins can have complex needs. They don't really like to be handled, and they may bite and scratch.

21

Snakes and lizards

Snakes and lizards are reptiles. They have dry, scaly skin and cannot make their own body heat. They are not as cuddly as some of the other animals that we share our homes with, but they make fascinating pets.

Reptiles are often kept in enclosures called terrariums or vivariums

WHERE THEY LIVE

In the wild, reptiles adapt to very specific conditions. To keep pet reptiles happy and healthy, we must recreate these conditions in enclosures with carefully controlled temperature, humidity, and UV light levels.

WHAT THEY EAT

Snakes are carnivores. What they eat depends on the species of snake, but varies from mice and birds to insects and worms. They swallow their food whole. Lizards can be herbivores, carnivores, or omnivores.

Food whole in snake's belly

Snakes
Snakes have long, thin bodies and no legs. They keep growing their whole lives.

Snakeskin
Snakes' skin becomes too small as they get bigger. Every few months, they shed their outer layer of skin to make room to grow.

Lizards
Most lizards walk about on four legs. They have ear holes on the sides of their heads.

Keeping lizards

Lizards can be a little more interactive than snakes. With a bit of time and effort you may even be able to teach your lizard some games and tricks.

Corn snake

Keeping snakes

The trickiest part of keeping a snake as a pet is getting its living conditions just right at the beginning. But once its home is set up, your slithery friend won't be very demanding.

Blue-tongued skink

JESS'S TIP

Some lizards need lots of space to roam around. Ask a professional how big your lizard will become when fully grown, and check that you will have room to care for it.

I love having vines and branches to climb!

Rat snake

Leopard gecko

Ball python

Bearded dragon

JESS'S TIP

When setting up for a snake, take plenty of time to research the temperature and humidity your specific snake species prefers, what type of bedding it needs, and how much lighting it likes.

California king snake

Crested gecko

Many snakes only need to be fed once a week and only poo once after each meal!

Iguana

23

Invertebrates

Invertebrates are animals without backbones and include insects and spiders. They often take up less space than other pets. They are fun to watch, but don't expect cuddles - invertebrates are often delicate and easily hurt.

Millipedes
Giant millipedes are calm critters with hundreds of tiny legs - all the better to tickle you with!

JESS'S TIP

Be sure to check that your invertebrate pet was bred in captivity, not taken from the wild. Never release a pet invertebrate into the wild.

Praying mantis

These animals are named for their front legs that they hold as if in prayer. They are incredible hunters. Like most insects, their life cycle starts with eggs. Females sometimes gobble up the head of mates to get important energy to produce eggs.

Female mantis

Tiny babies hatching

Hard case of the ootheca

Male mantis

1 Mating
A male and female praying mantis come together to mate. The female is often much bigger than the male.

2 Ootheca
The female then lays an eggsac called an ootheca. Its hard casing protects the young as they develop.

3 Hatching
Up to hundreds of tiny praying mantis babies hatch out of the ootheca, ready to venture out into the world on their own.

Leaf insects

Delicate leaf and stick insects can be very simple to keep. This makes them the perfect pets for people who don't have much spare time.

Spiders

Some spiders have venomous bites, others have harmful defensive tactics, and others have specific requirements for keeping them. Make sure you get specialist advice when choosing these creepy crawlies as pets.

Ants

A colony of ants can keep you entertained for hours! If you keep them in a glass or clear plastic enclosure, you will be able to see right inside their nest and watch them busily working away.

Giant snails

Giant snails can grow bigger than your fist! But if they escape, they can damage crops, so in some countries it is illegal to keep them as pets.

Snails can be kept alone or in groups.

Birds

Meet all my different bird buddies!

Clever, entertaining, and loving, birds can make incredible pets if they are kept well. Birds tend to need a lot of space to fly and can make quite a racket, so these feathery friends won't fit into every home.

CHITTER!
CHATTER!

Budgies

These little chatterboxes hold the record for the greatest number of words spoken by a pet bird.

African grey parrot

In captivity, African grey parrots have been known to live for an incredible 80 years. They often form a strong bond with their favourite person.

Ducks

Ducklings are very cute! However, remember that they quickly grow into big ducks that need a lot of space and a large area of water.

Chickens

Famous for producing tasty eggs, chickens make great pets! They can be trained easily and enjoy cuddles.

WING CLIPPING

Sometimes, a bird's wings are clipped to stop it flying away. This prevents it from acting like a normal bird, which can cause it distress.

TWEET!
TWEET!

Canary

Pet canaries come in many colours. Their enchanting songs have made them popular pets since the 17th century.

Cockatiels

The clowns of the bird world, cockatiels are cheeky, cheerful, affectionate, and cuddly.

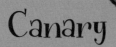

I love to fly and explore new places.

Lovebirds

One of the smallest types of parrot, lovebirds are active and curious. They often bond in pairs.

History

In Ancient Greece and Rome, brightly coloured birds were prized by wealthy families. The birds were often taken from the wild and kept in very small, highly decorated cages. These days, we are much better at caring for our feathery friends.

Animals with jobs

For a lot of animals, giving daily cuddles, playing with toys, and lounging around the house is top of the agenda. Others have important jobs to do, helping out humans and keeping us safe.

> I help to make the world a safer place for my human.

Sniffer dogs

With their super-sensitive noses, smart dogs can be trained to sniff out anything from dangerous explosives to illegal drugs.

Guide dogs

People who are partially sighted or blind can use specially trained guide dogs to navigate around people and objects. This allows them to do things they would find tricky to do on their own.

Truffle hunters

Pigs have an excellent sense of smell. They are experts at rooting out truffles, a type of stinky fungi that many humans love to eat, buried deep underground.

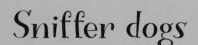

Goat gardeners

Many vineyards, where grapes are grown to be made into wine, use herds of goats to trim the grass instead of lawnmowers!

Guard llamas

Across the world, alpacas and llamas are used to guard farm animals such as sheep, hens, and turkeys. They protect them from predators such as wolves and coyotes.

Our protective nature makes us excellent guards.

Rescue dogs

Search and rescue dogs are trained to find people that are missing, trapped, or in danger. They work in many challenging conditions, such as in snow and underwater.

Ferret electricians

With long, thin bodies and a passion for scrambling through small spaces, ferrets are brilliant at helping humans thread cables underground and through walls.

A happy home

What makes your home a happy one? Most likely it's a mix of lots of different things, from having nice food to eat and your favourite pictures on your wall, to having the people you love around you. What do you think pets need?

Just like us, our animal family members need more than just basic living conditions to have a happy life.

IMAGINE...

Think about how you would feel if you were only allowed to stay in one room, with no toys, blankets, or decorations. Imagine if you weren't allowed to have friends to visit and you had the same food for every meal. Would you be happy?

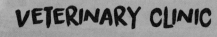

HOME

PARK

VETERINARY CLINIC

Act natural
To be happy, normal animals, pets should be allowed to behave naturally. If they like to be alone, they shouldn't be forced to live in a group. If they like to live in groups, they will be lonely if they are kept on their own. If they like to run, they should have enough space to do so. And if they like to hide, then shelters will make them feel safe.

A safe space
It's important for pets to be given the right type of home that keeps them safe. It should always be kept clean and comfortable, with plenty of room for them to move around.

Pets should be up-to-date with their vet visits and taken to the vets if they show any signs of illness or pain.

Food and drink
Pets must always have access to fresh water and should be given the right type of food at the right times of day.

Happy brains
Many pets like to use their brains a lot, but others don't. For some pets, keeping their brains happy might involve playing games and having cuddles. For others, having a happy brain may mean being able to hide away and rest, without the fear of being chased or picked up.

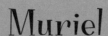

Would any of us be happy in your home?

The right animal for your family

Each animal needs something different from its family, depending on factors such as its age, personality, or size.

Muriel

Quiet stick insect seeking a warm family home and a regular supply of fresh leaves.

Ted

Energetic puppy seeking a family that loves walking and doesn't mind the occasional chewed shoe.

We older pets like to have plenty of rest.

Rosie and Chick

Noisy chicken and fluffy chick seeking an outdoor home with other chickens, safely away from hungry foxes. Will provide fresh eggs.

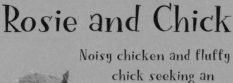

Frank

Old, gentle cat seeking a quiet home with no other pets. Particularly fond of a warm lap to sit on in the evenings.

32

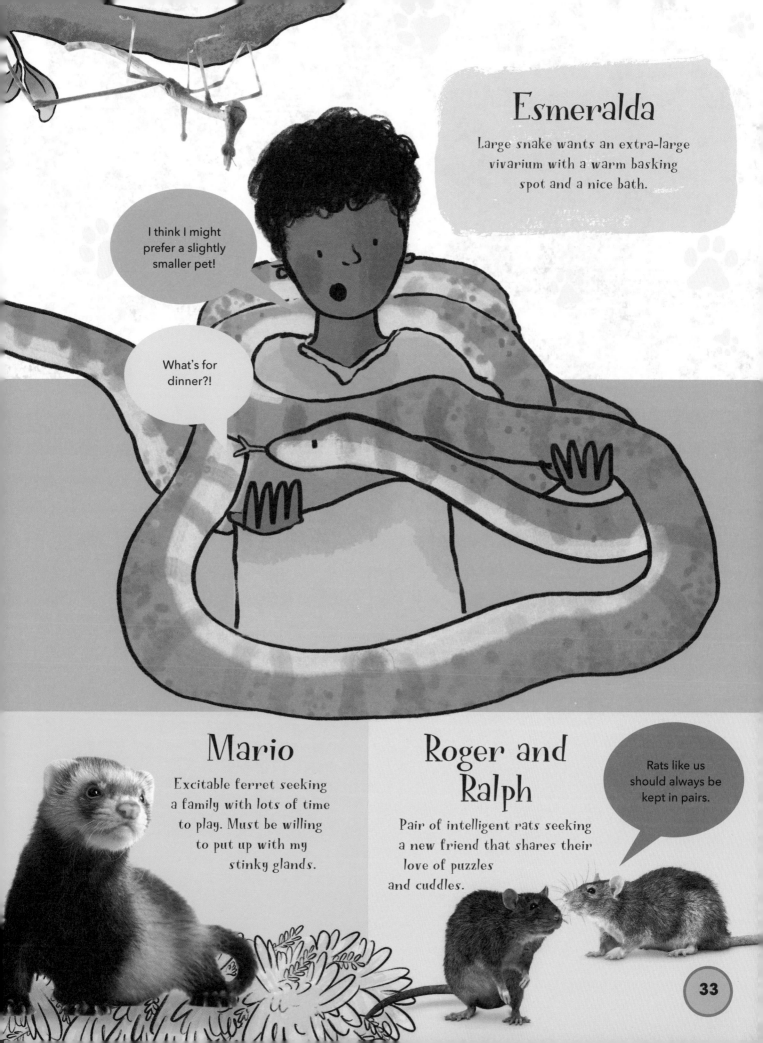

Getting your pet

If you've decided that you have enough time, money, and space to care for a pet and you have worked out which kind of animal will be most happy in your home, the next step is to find your new best friend!

Give an animal a second chance at a happy home by adopting it.

PET RESCUE CENTRE

ADOPT, DON'T SHOP

There are thousands of animals waiting in rescue centres to be adopted. Often they have lost their homes through no fault of their own and they are just waiting to be part of a family again.

The first visit

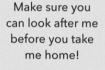

If you are getting your pet from a breeder, always visit the pet in their own home. If it is a young animal, ask if you can see both parents. Never take a pet away on the first visit – this is your chance to get to know one another and see if you are a good match. Take the opportunity to ask questions and make sure there are no obvious problems.

Make sure you can look after me before you take me home!

JESS'S TIP

You are responsible for caring for your pet, so expect the breeder or rescue centre to ask questions about you too! They care about their animals, so will want to know they are going to a good home.

Picking the right pet

Rescue centres have animals of all sorts of ages and breeds. You can meet and get to know lots of different animals before deciding which one you think would be happy in your home.

Pet care

Rescue centres can also give you lots of advice on how to care for your pet properly. They will even help you if you have any problems after taking your pet home.

COSTS

- Veterinary care
- Vaccinations
- Food and bedding
- Insurance
- Toys
- Training classes
- Pet sitters

35

Growing up

Sometimes, pets come into our homes when they are *still* babies. They may be frightened at first, but if you treat them gently and kindly, they will soon settle into the family.

New to the world

Some newborn animals are able to look after themselves as soon as they are born. Others, such as cats, are completely helpless and rely on their mothers to look after them.

I lick my kittens regularly to keep them clean. It also helps them pass waste.

BIRTH

When kittens are born, their eyes are closed and their ears are folded shut. They rely on their mum for everything.

FOUR DAYS

After just four days, kittens have already grown a lot. They use their senses of taste and smell to explore the world around them.

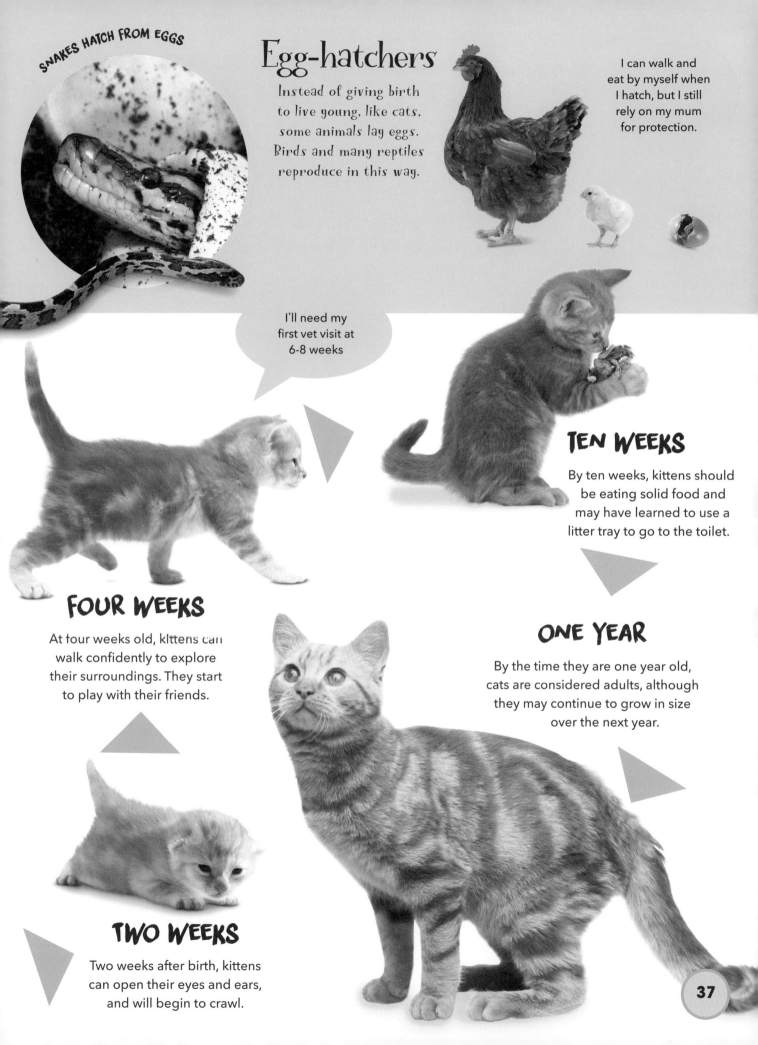

Egg-hatchers

Instead of giving birth to live young, like cats, some animals lay eggs. Birds and many reptiles reproduce in this way.

I can walk and eat by myself when I hatch, but I still rely on my mum for protection.

I'll need my first vet visit at 6-8 weeks

TEN WEEKS

By ten weeks, kittens should be eating solid food and may have learned to use a litter tray to go to the toilet.

FOUR WEEKS

At four weeks old, kittens can walk confidently to explore their surroundings. They start to play with their friends.

ONE YEAR

By the time they are one year old, cats are considered adults, although they may continue to grow in size over the next year.

TWO WEEKS

Two weeks after birth, kittens can open their eyes and ears, and will begin to crawl.

37

How long do pets live?

While most of the animals we keep as pets are unlikely to live for more than 20 years, some do live longer. Parrots and tortoises have both been known to live to be over 100!

In general, smaller animals live shorter lives than larger ones.

Praying mantis
Some praying mantises live for just a few months. Females often survive longer than males.

Hamster
When carefully looked after, hamsters can live for about two or three years. Some rare individuals have made it to the age of seven!

Mouse
Everything happens fast in the life of a mouse – at just six weeks old, a mouse can even have babies of its own! A pet mouse generally lives for about two years.

UP TO **1 YEAR**   UP TO **3 YEARS**   UP TO **4 YEARS**   UP TO **7 YEARS**

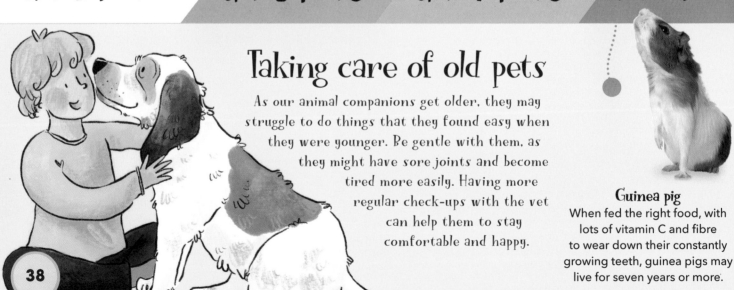

Taking care of old pets

As our animal companions get older, they may struggle to do things that they found easy when they were younger. Be gentle with them, as they might have sore joints and become tired more easily. Having more regular check-ups with the vet can help them to stay comfortable and happy.

Guinea pig
When fed the right food, with lots of vitamin C and fibre to wear down their constantly growing teeth, guinea pigs may live for seven years or more.

IN THE WILD

Animals tend to have much shorter lives in the wild. They face many more threats to their survival, including predators, diseases, and dangerous weather conditions, than pets do.

One year of a dog's life is equivalent to seven human ones!

Cat

Some cats manage to live into their twenties, but the average lifespan of a domestic cat is 14 years.

Tarantula

It might be hard to believe, but one of the longest-living pets you can welcome into your home is a spider. Tarantulas can live for as many as 30 years!

Dog

Different breeds of dogs have slightly different life expectancies. Around 10–13 years is considered a good average age for a dog, but some dogs live for much longer.

UP TO 12 YEARS   UP TO 18 YEARS   UP TO 30 YEARS

Rabbit

n the wild, rabbits often ie before they turn three. However, in our homes, safe from predators and looked after by loving humans, they can live for more than ten years!

When a pet dies

Most pets won't live for as long as we do, and one day they will die. While this is a normal part of life, it is still very sad. It can help to remember our pets through stories, photographs, and the memories we shared when they were alive.

You could plant a tree to remember your pet by

Visiting the vet

If you have a pet, before long you will need to take it to visit a vet. Vets are animal doctors, who help us to keep our pets healthy. If our pets are ever poorly, vets will try to make them better.

Vet

Veterinary surgeons (vets) are experts in animal bodies and are taught how to fix them if something goes wrong.

Nurse

Veterinary nurses help vets to look after our pets. They are highly trained, important members of the team.

WHEN SHOULD YOU VISIT A VET?

Any time your pet is acting unusually, it's a good idea to take it to the vet for a check.

Healthy pets often come to the vets too!

PUPPY TRAINING CLASSES

Training classes are great for socializing your puppy.

Check for fleas!

Vets provide flea and worm treatments.

Health checks
Get very old and very young pets checked regularly, even when they seem okay.

VETERINARY CLINIC

Vets can give injured pets medicine for pain relief and can treat their wounds.

Vaccinate your pet

Injury
Pets come to the vets if they are injured.

Keep pet teeth healthy

Make sure you keep your pet's teeth clean.

Weighing
Vets weigh pets to check they're not losing or gaining too much weight.

An electronic device (a microchip) containing details of their owner can be added to pets in case they get lost.

GET MICROCHIPPED NOW!

Nail clipping
Sometimes pets visit the vets to have their nails trimmed.

JESS'S TIP

Emergency vets are available 24 hours a day, 365 days a year. Keep a note of the phone number for your nearest emergency vet, just in case.

41

Poorly pets

You know your pet better than anyone, so you know what is normal for them and what is not. If you notice something has changed and it's making you worried, the best thing to do is get it checked out by a vet.

Watch out for changes in appetite

Drinking more

There are lots of reasons why pets might suddenly start to drink more water. For example, the weather could be hot or they may have a new type of food. But if your pet is drinking more and there's no clear reason why, it could be a sign of illness.

Pay attention to how much I drink.

Some cats are fussy drinkers

Eating differently

Keep an eye on any change in your pet's appetite, whether they are eating more or eating less. Lots of things can affect how much your pet eats though, including how much it likes its food!

Pick up your pet's poo!

Poo

You can tell a lot from your pet's poo. If it becomes particularly watery or contains blood, something could be wrong.

Let's take you for a check-up to be safe.

Body changes

Giving your pet regular strokes and cuddles will help you to spot if there are ever any changes on their body. Any new lumps, bumps, or changes to your pet's skin should be checked by a vet.

Ooooooooh, that's better!

Itching

If your pet is itching, the first thing to check is if they are up to date with their flea treatment.

Sleeping

Sleeping more can be normal as your pets get older. Some animals also sleep more than others. However, if their habits seem unusual, talk to a vet.

JESS'S TIP

You are the expert on your pet. If something seems wrong, even if you can't put your finger on exactly what, trust your instincts and take it to the vet.

Changes in personality

Sometimes your pet just doesn't seem quite right. If your pet is not acting normally, it could be because they are in pain or feeling unwell. Take them to the vet to put your mind at ease.

I don't feel well. My head hurts when I move.

I don't wake up until the Sun goes down.

Communication

Do you listen to what your pet is telling you? They can't use words, but pets have plenty of other ways of showing us how they feel.

Tail wagging happy ....

Sniffing

When dogs meet, they can learn lots about one another just by giving each other a good sniff!

DOG SOUNDS

Dogs can make lots of different sounds, from barks and yelps to howls and whines. Each noise means something different and it's worth spending some time learning to understand them.

WHINE!

Tail down, crouching

Crouching
A crouched body and tucked tail says "I'm scared".

.. **Eyes downcast**

Posture

A dog's posture can tell you if it is frightened, relaxed, angry, or playful. Is it crouched low or standing tall? Is its coat flat or are its hackles raised? What is it doing with its ears, eyes, and tail?

Teeth bared ..

GROWL!

Growling
Growling is a dog's way of telling you that it has had enough. Don't tell a dog off for growling – it may learn not to warn you in future and to move straight to biting.

BARK!

Ears

Ears come in handy for more than just hearing - they also show how an animal is feeling. Pricked up ears usually mean an animal is alert, and flattened ears can mean an animal is angry or afraid.

WOOF!

MEW!

HISS!

Scent

Cats use their scent glands to send messages to other cats nearby, without having to meet them.

Prey animals

It can be harder to read the body language of rabbits and guinea pigs. In the wild, it could be dangerous for them to show weakness.

CAT SOUNDS

All cats can make a wide variety of sounds to tell you how they're feeling. Some breeds, such as Siamese and Burmese cats, are chattier than others.

MEOW!

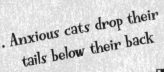
.... Anxious cats drop their tails below their back

Tail bristled in anger or fear ......

Tail up, content .....

Telling tails

A happy cat will carry its tail high, sometimes with a curl in the tip. A moving tail is a sign that a cat is alert and could be irritated. The faster a cat's tail is moving, the more agitated it is feeling.

Learning the rules

When we bring animals into our human world, they have no idea how we expect them to act. Teaching them basic rules and working together to learn new tricks is not only fun, but it can keep them safe too.

We make a great team!

Record breakers

Alex, an African grey parrot, could name items by their shape and colour. This had never been done before by a bird!

Alexis, an Austrian cat, broke the record for the most tricks performed in a minute – she achieved 26 tricks.

Chaser the dog has been taught the names of 1,022 items – more than any other animal. She can also sort them into groups, such as shape, something children learn to do around the age of three.

PET PRAISE

The best way to train any pet is to reward them when they do something you want them to do and ignore them when they do something you don't want them to do.

Toilet training

Some pets can be taught to use a litter tray, so they don't make a mess in the house or in their enclosure. These include ferrets, rabbits, cats, guinea pigs, and rats.

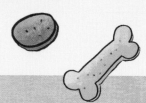

GOOD BOY!

If your pet uses the litter tray, reward it with lots of praise.

BASIC COMMANDS FOR YOUR DOG

SIT!

"Sit" is one of the easiest commands to teach. Start with this.

LIE DOWN!

"Lie down" can be a trickier command for dogs to master.

STAY!

Once they obey "Sit", try getting your dog to stay there.

COME!

Teach your dog to come when called, so it returns when you're out.

DROP!

"Drop" can stop dogs picking up things they shouldn't.

Puppy socialization

There is a special window of time in a puppy's life, between the ages of four weeks and 12 weeks, called the socialization period. This is when a puppy's brain learns about new things. It's really important to let your pup experience lots of different things during this time so they get used to different sounds, smells, people, animals, and places.

This is a fun toy!

What's this? It smells nice!

Play time!

In the wild, animals are always on the go. There is lots to do, from searching for food and making their homes to being ready to run away from danger. Although our pets don't have to hunt, build, or flee from danger, it's still important for them to be active.

KEEP IT NATURAL

Learn about how your pet would act in the wild and try to play games that allow them to practise those same actions and skills.

Fetch
Dogs love to play fetch, chasing after a ball and bringing it back to you.

> Playing fetch is fun for me, and means I bond with my human too!

Running
Exercise wheels can help your pet get the activity it needs. Make sure the wheel has a solid floor that won't catch your pet's toes. Don't use exercise balls as your pet cannot escape when it is feeling tired.

Flying
Make sure pet birds are given plenty of time to stretch their wings outside of their cages.

Climbing

Boxes, ladders, branches, and ropes make perfect climbing frames for mice and rats.

We need lots of time to play outside our cages.

Bathing

Taking a dust bath isn't just great fun for a chinchilla – it keeps their skin and fur healthy too.

I love to bring you toys as gifts.

Chasing

For animals that hunt, such as cats and dogs, chasing toys is a natural instinct.

Safety first

Make sure the toys you use are designed for pets and do not have any parts that can be easily bitten off or swallowed.

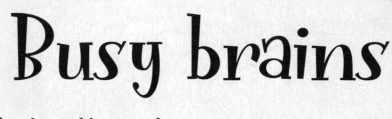

Busy brains

In the wild, animals aren't given their food in a bowl - they have to work for it! It's important that we encourage our pets to use their brains like they would in the wild to stop them getting bored.

Branch to climb

GIVE A SNAKE LEVELS TO EXPLORE

Snakes

Keep your snake interested by giving it new toys and things to climb, and moving objects around in its enclosure.

Dogs

Daily walks and playdates with other dogs are brilliant for your dog's brain, but you can encourage them to use their brain at home too.

Snuffle mat
Scatter some treats on a snuffle mat - your dog will have to work hard to find them among the mat's strands.

Rabbits

Make mealtimes a game! Instead of putting your rabbit's pellets in a pile, hide them inside tunnels or bury them in hay.

Hidden treasure
Stuff herbs and hay inside an old kitchen roll or paper bag.

Puzzle feeder
Use a puzzle feeder to release food slowly and keep your dog's brain active.

Ball puzzle feeder

Treat toy
Rabbits are naturally inquisitive and love to explore new toys such as puzzles. Have a look in your local pet shop.

KEEP RABBITS INTERESTED WITH PUZZLES

50

Hang vegetables on a string

Chickens

Hang vegetables such as broccoli, carrots, mushrooms, and beets from string to keep chickens entertained.

HIDE BERRIES AROUND THE COOP

Lizards

Twist flexible vines around your lizard's habitat for it to climb.

LIZARDS LOVE TO CLIMB BRANCHES

Flexible vine

Cats

Some cats go outside, where the whole world is their playground! But there are items you can get to stimulate your cat's brain indoors too.

I love to hunt for toys and food.

JESS'S TIP

Some owners entertain their pets while they're out by leaving the TV or radio on.

Activity centre

Hanging toys

Puzzle feeder

Grooming

...ed more help than others to keep their coats ...and tidy, but for all animals, grooming can be a great way for you to bond with your pet. It can also give you a chance to check them for lumps, bumps, and scrapes.

Dog hair

Dog hair can be curly or straight, long or short, thick or thin. Some dogs may need daily brushing to keep their coat healthy, whereas others can go for weeks without seeing a comb. Professional groomers can help you to keep tricky tangles under control.

....Dog claws

Dog claws

Dog claws are usually worn down by walking on hard ground. However, if you think your dog's claws have grown too long, visit a groomer or vet for advice. If your dog's claws need regular trimming, a professional can teach you how to cut them safely.

Dog bath

If your dog rolls in something stinky, you may need to wash it - make sure to use a shampoo that is safe for pets.

Groomer

Pet-safe shampoo

If you notice bald patches, redness, or flaky skin, take me to the vet.

Cat hair

Young, short-haired cats are usually very good at grooming themselves using their rough tongues, but long-haired or older cats may need a helping hand.

Cat claws

Cats usually wear their claws down themselves out and about or on a scratching post. They also shed (allow to fall off) their claw sheaths, the dry, outer layer of their claws, which helps their claws grow.

Horse grooming

Grooming a horse is a big job! As well as brushing the whole body, mane, and tail, the hooves must be "picked out" with a hooked instrument called a hoof pick to remove mud and stones.

HOOF PICKING

Small furries

It is important to brush long-haired rabbits and guinea pigs to prevent their fur matting (getting tangled), and to stop poo getting stuck in it.

Brush me gently as my skin is sensitive!

Saying hello!

Humans often greet one another with a wave, a hug, or a kiss on the cheek. Our pets don't usually do those things, so how do we know if they are happy to see us?

POPCORNING IS A SIGN OF A HAPPY GUINEA PIG

Dogs

Dogs bark excitedly and wag their tails when they see people they know. When you meet a new dog, check with the owner first that you can touch them. Then offer your hand to say hello but avoid patting them on the top of the head.

Guinea pigs

When a guinea pig is very happy or excited, it may make a sudden leap very high into the air. This is known as "popcorning".

Cats

If they are pleased to see you, cats may rub you with their cheeks or wind their way between your legs.

Ferrets

Friendly ferrets will show you how much they love you by licking you on your arms and hands. Ferrets love to give their owners these little "kisses".

Ferret ....

Rabbit talk

Rabbits mostly use their bodies to tell humans how they feel.

Happy rabbits will run in circles around your feet to show you affection.

A rabbit will flop down in front of you if they trust you.

Birds

Some birds sing and dance when they see the humans they love. Others use their beaks to groom their favourite people, which is called preening.

CHIRP!

CHIRP!

Territorial rabbits

Rabbits also use their bodies to communicate with other rabbits.

Rabbits will rub their chin on items to send other rabbits the message: "That's mine!".

Rabbits will lick one another to show who's boss.

What's for dinner?

Just like humans, our pets must eat the right food each day to stay healthy. But the foods they need to eat - and how often they should eat them - can be very different!

MENU

Guinea pigs
Guinea pigs must have food that's made especially for them, which contains extra vitamin C.

Dogs
Domestic dogs have evolved alongside humans, eating our scraps, so they are very good at digesting plants and cereals, as well as meat.

Horses
Horses love to munch on grass or hay. They should eat about one per cent of their body weight in this food a day.

Kittens
Young animals must eat food that contains extra calories and the right vitamins and fatty acids so they can develop properly.

Dogs are omnivores, which means we eat both meat and plants.

Choosing the right food for your animal

It is important to feed your animal companion a food that is designed for their species, so that it contains all the right proteins, nutrients, and other minerals in the perfect amounts.

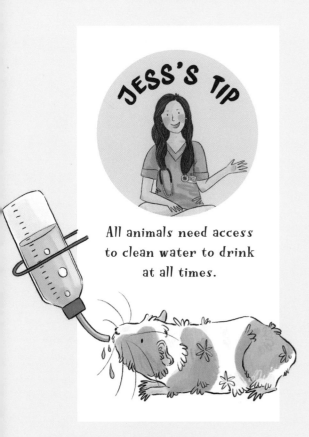

All animals need access to clean water to drink at all times.

The right amount

Being overweight is a big problem for pets - it puts extra pressure on their hearts, bones, and joints, and can make them more likely to get certain diseases. But not giving your pet enough to eat also has its share of problems. Most animal foods have guides on the packet that show you how much you should feed your pet each day.

·····Too much?

····· Too little?

POISONOUS FOODS

Just because a food is safe for humans to eat, it doesn't mean we should share it with our pets. Many common foods can be poisonous for our furry friends.

All forms of chocolate are toxic to dogs, including cocoa powder and chocolate bars.

Onions are poisonous to most pets, including dogs, cats, and rabbits.

Grapes can make dogs and cats very ill.

The whole of the lily plant, inluding its pollen, is toxic to cats.

Garlic is toxic for many pets.

Xylitol is a sweetener found in chewing gum and medications. It is harmless to people but very toxic to dogs.

Corn on the cob could be swallowed and get stuck inside a pet's digestive system.

In all weathers

Come rain or shine, your pet relies on you, so don't let the weather keep you from cleaning, feeding, and exercising your furry friend.

Beat the chill with a warm jacket, hat, and gloves.

Wear bright or reflective clothing when walking in the dark.

Short-haired dogs may need coats to keep warm in winter.

NEVER WALK ON ICY FROZEN LAKES WITH DOGS

Freezing over
In winter months, drinking water may freeze, so check your pet's water regularly. Cold air can feel chilly even for the furriest of creatures.

In the cold

Fit a catflap
If your cat likes to be outside, make sure it has a catflap. This means it can access the indoors, where it can be protected from the cold.

Warm up enclosures
Help rabbits and guinea pigs by giving them extra straw, insulating their house, and adding a blanket to cover the home overnight.

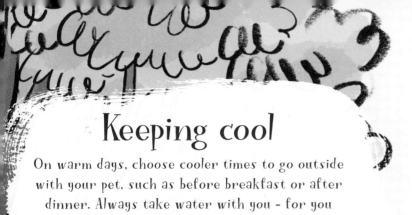

Keeping cool

On warm days, choose cooler times to go outside with your pet, such as before breakfast or after dinner. Always take water with you - for you and your pet!

Skip walks when it's too hot

Icy relief
Adding an ice cube to your dog's water bowl will make it extra refreshing and offer relief from the heat.

MAKE SURE YOUR PET'S WATER IS ALWAYS TOPPED UP

In the heat

Make shelter in the shade
Make sure rabbit and guinea pig houses are in a shady part of the garden, or away from windows if they are inside.

Test the pavement
Dogs don't have shoes to protect their feet, so feel the ground with your hand. If it's too hot for your hand, then it's too hot for your dog's paws.

Stay out of hot cars
Never leave your pet in the car on a hot day. The temperature inside can quickly rise to dangerous levels, and your pet may overheat.

Staying safe

When we welcome animals into our families, they become our responsibility. As well as providing them with food, fresh water, shelter, and love, it is our duty to keep them safe from harm.

Report bad treatment

If you are worried about an animal, or you see a pet being treated badly, tell a grown up. Charities such as the RSPCA investigate animal cruelty.

DOGS SHOULD NOT BE LEFT IN HOT CARS

Out and about

If your dog hasn't learned to come back when you call them, or if you're walking somewhere unfamiliar, it's safer to keep them on a lead.

WHEN YOU MEET A DOG

- Ask the owner if it is ok to say hello.

- Offer your hand for the dog to sniff before stroking them.

- Don't approach a new dog if their human is not around.

Dogs still enjoy walks even if they are on the lead.

Rabbit responsibilities

In the wild, rabbits escape from predators by darting underground. When we keep rabbits in enclosures at home, they don't have underground tunnels to keep them safe, so it's our responsibility to protect them.

Rabbit hutch

Predator proof
Rabbit houses and runs must keep out predators such as foxes and birds of prey.

Living space
Make sure your rabbit hutch or run has enough space for your rabbit to run around safely, especially if you are keeping more than one rabbit.

DANGEROUS SUBSTANCES

Many of the things we use for cleaning our homes can be dangerous to pets. They must be kept locked away, well out of their reach.

Antifreeze is deadly to cats

Make sure electrical wires can't be chewed

61

Pet people

There are lots of incredible people who work with pets to make their lives better and happier. Here are some of them. Would you like to do any of these jobs one day?

Dog trainer

Dog trainers are experts at teaching people and their dogs how to work together and learn new tricks.

Groomer

Groomers help us to keep our pets clean and tidy. They have lo of special equipment especially for pampering our pets.

Behaviourist

Sometimes our pets act in ways that we struggle to understand. A behaviourist can help us get to the bottom of how our pets are feeling.

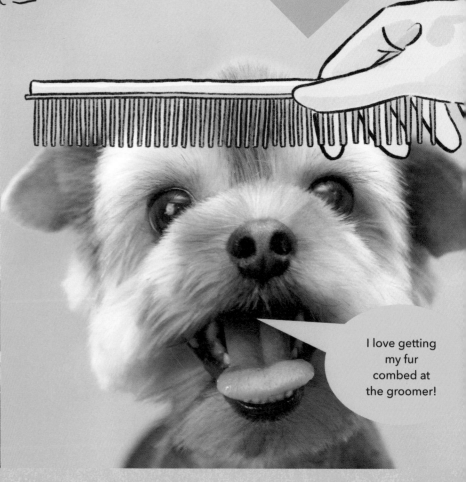

I love getting my fur combed at the groomer!

Care giver

Animal care givers work in rescue centres and veterinary practices. They give food, water, and cuddles to pets, clean and groom them, and keep their homes clean and tidy.

Nutritionist

Pet nutritionists make sure pets eat all the ingredients they need to stay healthy.

Pet shop assistant

People who work in pet shops look after animals until they find owners, and make sure they are going to a happy home.

Dog walker

It's not always possible for dog owners to give their dogs as much exercise as they need. Dog walkers help out by walking their dogs for them.

I love being outside with my furry friends.

Animal rescue

Specially trained animal rescuers investigate reports of animals that are injured or in danger. They work with a team to save them.

No pet? No problem!

What if a pet won't fit into your family? Can you *still* spend time with animals? Of course you can! The world is full of incredible creatures. In fact, they are all around us if we look hard enough. Here are some of the animal encounters that are waiting on our doorsteps.

Squirrel house

HELPING WILD ANIMALS

We share our world with wild animals that need our help just as much as pets do. Remember, before our houses were built, the land belonged to wild animals, and it was much easier for them to safely explore and find food. So how can you help the animals in your patch?

JESS'S TIP

Having a pet is hard work! If you know somebody with one, why not offer to help from time to time? Maybe they need someone to look after their guinea pig while they go on holiday, or take their dog for extra walks.

Put out food

You can feed wild animals in all sorts of different ways. You could hang up feeders for birds, but avoid those that are made from netting. Start leaving out cat food for hedgehogs. Or even grow flowers to feed nectar-loving insects.

Farms and stables

Is there a farm or stable near you? They can be great places to meet bigger animals such as horses, cows, sheep, and pigs. They may even appreciate a little help if you're keen to get involved.

Get outside!

One of the easiest ways to spend time with animals is to get outside. There is so much wildlife to see. Remember, though, that most of the animals you see are wild and should be watched from a distance.

Bird box

Bird boxes are often placed on the sides of buildings and trees. Watch them for signs of activity.

Bug hotel

Look under rocks and logs to find minibeasts. You could even make them a bug hotel.

Visit shelter dogs

While they are waiting for new homes, dogs in shelters can get lonely. Why not talk to an adult and offer to go in and read books to the dogs? The sound of your voice could be comforting, and you may even get a dog snuggle in return!

> I love listening to you reading to me! It makes me feel calm and happy.

Pond life

BINOCULARS HELP YOU SPOT ANIMALS THAT ARE FAR AWAY

If you stare out of the window for long enough, you are bound to spot some local wildlife. If you want to meet some of the more shy species, however, you need to put in a bit more effort. Hides are shelters out in the wild that allow you to watch animals without them seeing you and being disturbed.

Animals in the wild

We aren't only responsible for looking after pets - we must also care for animals in the wild. It may not seem like it, but the decisions we make each day impact creatures all over the world, so it's up to us to make the right ones.

Protect the oceans

Marine animals can end up eating or getting tangled in plastic we throw away. Reduce the amount of plastic you use, and reuse and recycle it when you can.

I prefer an ocean free from plastic waste!

Eat less meat

Try going meat-free for some of your meals. If you have a garden, you could even have a go at growing your own vegetables!

Combat climate change

Try walking or cycling instead of taking the car and switch off lights when you leave a room to save energy.

Take a bike to help stop our home melting!

Tigers are endangered ....

Sponsor an endangered animal

Give money to a charity that is working to protect animals that are endangered because of human actions. Some will even let you choose an animal to sponsor.

Orangutan habitats are threatened

Save the rainforests

Look out for symbols that show the products you are buying have not caused harm to rainforests.

Plant trees

Work with your community to plant trees and other plants in your area. They can help by absorbing climate-changing gases from the atmosphere.

.... Books

Learn

Take time to learn about the issues faced by the animals in our world. Read books, watch documentaries, and ask questions.

I love talking about the ways we can protect animals.

Use your voice

Tell your friends and family all about the issues faced by animals and the planet. Encourage them to make positive changes with you.

67

Glossary

adapt
How a living thing changes over time to help it survive better in its environment

breed
Variety of a pet or farm animal; for example, a collie is a breed of dog

captivity
When animals are kept in a certain place by humans

carnivore
Animal that eats meat

climate change
Change in temperature and weather across the Earth that can be natural or caused by human activity

command
Order that tells an animal to do something; for example, "Sit!"

domestic
Animals kept as pets or on farms

endangered
Animal or plant species that is in danger of becoming extinct

gland
Part of the body that makes particular chemicals

hackles
Hairs along an animal's neck or back, which lift up when it is angry or scared

herbivore
Animal that eats only plants

hide
Shelter in the wild that is often camouflaged, and can be used to watch animals, especially birds, without disturbing them

humidity
Amount of water vapour in the air, which makes it feel moist

insulate
Protect an object from heat or cold by adding material

invertebrate
Animal that does not have a spine, such as an insect, worm, jellyfish, or spider

marine
To do with the sea

mummify
Dry and wrap a body to preserve it and make it into a mummy

omnivore
Animal that eats both plants and meat

protractile
Able to be pushed out

reproduce
Produce children

socializing
Spending time with other animals

sponsor
Give money to a charity to take care of an animal

stimulate
Make active or excited

terrarium
See-through enclosure for keeping small animals such as turtles

toxic
Substance that is dangerous, such as poison

vaccinate
Give an injection to protect against infection or disease

vivarium
See-through enclosure for keeping animals such as snakes and lizards

warren
Network of animal burrows

Index

Acknowledgements

The publisher would like to thank the following people for their assistance in making this book: Clare Lloyd for editorial help, Sunita Gahir for design help, Ruth McDonald for consulting, and Susie Rae for proofreading and indexing.

The publisher would like to thank the following for their kind permission to reproduce their photographs:

(Key: a-above; b-below/bottom; c-centre; f-far; l-left; r-right; t-top)

2 123RF.com: Naphazynths Chanthvongsviriya (tr). **6 Depositphotos Inc:** Judithdz (cl). **Dorling Kindersley:** Peter Anderson / Odds Farm Park, High Wycombe, Bucks (ca). **Dreamstime.com:** Isselee (c); Eric Isselee (cr, bl). **Getty Images / iStock:** Stepanyda (bc). **7 Dorling Kindersley:** Paul Dykes / West Sussex Beekeepers Association (bl). **Dreamstime.com:** Anankkml (cla); Jon Helgason (cr); Liliia Khuzhakhmetova (ca); Alexander Potapov (bc). **Fotolia:** Stefan Andronache (1/bc). **Getty Images:** DigitalVision / Buena Vista Images (cl). **8 123RF.com:** Steve Byland (bc); Christian Musat (1/bc). **Dreamstime.com:** Anankkml (crb); Sonsedskaya (bl); Isselee (br, cb). **9 Dreamstime.com:** Auris (b); Jagodka (tl). **11 Alamy Stock Photo:** Alberto Ortega (ca). **Dreamstime.com:** Adogslifephoto (bc); Juhku (clb). **13 Alamy Stock Photo:** Bailey-Cooper Photography (tc); Blickwinkel / Fotototo (1/tc). **Dreamstime.com:** Anett Bakos (bl); Tevarak11 (crb). **Getty Images / iStock:** E+ / andresr (tl). **Shutterstock.com:** G_O_S (br). **14 123RF.com:** lapis2380 (cb/x3); vangert (cla); Prasit Supho (x3). **Dreamstime.com:** Mirkorosenau (crb/x3). **Fotolia:** L_amica (cb). **15 Dreamstime.com:** Bluehand (cb/x2, clb); Monika Wisniewska (cra); Isselee (cb/x5); Underworld (tl); Bogonet (tc); Tatus (clb/x2); Riefza (crb/x2). **Fotolia:** L_amica (cb). **16 Dreamstime.com:** Vitalij Geraskin (bl); Isselee (tr). **Getty Images / iStock:** GlobalP (br). **17 Dreamstime.com:** Subbotina (crb); Werg (cla). **18 123RF.com:** Naphazynths Chanthvongsviriya (r). **Alamy Stock Photo:** FLPA (bl). **Getty Images:** Moment / Jose A. Bernat Bacete (ca). **19 Dreamstime.com:** Nadmikusova (tl). **20 Dreamstime.com:** Auris (b); Isselee (cb). **21 Alamy Stock Photo:** Image Quest Marine / Justin Peach (tc); Petographer (tl); Gina Easley / Stockimo (1/tc). **Dorling Kindersley:** Twan Leenders (bl). **Dreamstime.com:** VetraKori (crb). **22 Dreamstime.com:** Eric Issele (clb); I Wayan Sumatika (br). **23 123RF.com:** Laurent Davoust (r). **Depositphotos Inc:** Luislouro (br). **Dreamstime.com:** Laura Cattrall (cl); Sasin Tipchai (tl); Farinoza (tc, crb); Matthijs Kuijpers (cl); Eastmanphoto (cr). **24-25 Dreamstime.com:** Alison Gibson. **24 Alamy Stock Photo:** Nature Picture Library / Alex Hyde (tr). **Getty Images / iStock:** Fotofrankyat (clb); Mohamed Haddad (cb). **naturepl.com:** Kim Taylor (br). **25 Dreamstime.com:** Ernest Cooper (c); Melinda Fawver (tc); Dm Stock Production (tr); Tatiana Kutina (b); Isselee (bl). **Getty Images:** Moment / Somnuk Krobkum (tl). **26 Alamy Stock Photo:** Blickwinkel / Maehrmann (cl); Juniors Bildarchiv GmbH / F240 (tl); Kay Roxby (br). **Dreamstime.com:** Isselee (cr); Valentina Razumova (clb). **Getty Images / iStock:** E+ / Georgeclerk (bl). **26-27 Dreamstime.com:** Alison Gibson. **27 Alamy Stock Photo:** Petra Wegner (cr). **Dreamstime.com:** Ian Dyball (tr); Isselee (cl). **28 123RF.com:** Monika Wisniewska (bl). **Dreamstime.com:** Julia Pfeifer (br). **Getty Images:** Foodcollection / StockFood (bc). **28-29 Dreamstime.com:** Alison Gibson. **29 Alamy Stock Photo:** DPA Picture Alliance / Jens Kalaene (tc); Krystyna Szulecka (cr). **30 Dreamstime.com:** Vasyl Helevachuk (cr); Isselee (bc). **Getty Images:** Moment / Sandra Clegg (bl). **31 123RF.com:** Michael Thompson (br). **Dreamstime.com:** Cynoclub (c); Mark Herreid (1/cla); Aleksandr Zyablitskiy (cra); Sergey Galushko (1/cra); Photodeti (ca); Isselee (clb). **Getty Images / iStock:** Elmvilla (cla). **32 123RF.com:** Mikkel Bigandt (cr). **Fotolia:** Eric Isselee (cla). **33 Dreamstime.com:** Isselee (bl). **34 Dreamstime.com:** Ievgen Cherniavskyi (cr). **Getty Images:** 500px / Andrs Lpez (bc); Stockbyte / Life On White (cb); Moment / Amy Lane Photography (br). **34-35 Dreamstime.com:** Viacheslav Dubrovin (b). **35 Alamy Stock Photo:** John Crowe (tl); Justin Ruscheinski / EyeEm (cb); Kritsada Yokubon / EyeEm (1/cb). **Dreamstime.com:** Isselee (ca). **Getty Images / iStock:** E+ / Vasiliki (bl).

36-37 Dreamstime.com: Alison Gibson; Brian Magnier (tc). **37 Alamy Stock Photo:** John Cancalosi (tl). **Dreamstime.com:** Wildlife World (cra). **Getty Images / iStock:** Stepanyda (tr). **38 Dreamstime.com:** Roxana Gonzalez (cl); Jagodka (1/cl); Isselee (br). **Getty Images / iStock:** Natalia Kopyltsova (cra). **39 Dreamstime.com:** Isselee (tl). **Getty Images / iStock:** GlobalP (tc, tr); MirekKijewski (cr). **40 123RF.com:** Kanoksak Tameeraksa (c). **Dreamstime.com:** Auris (crb); Alison Gibson (cl/x2); Bolotov (cr/x2); Erikreis (cr). **Getty Images / iStock:** E+ / PK-Photos (1/crb). **41 123RF.com:** Kanoksak Tameeraksa (x3). **Dreamstime.com:** Bolotov (cl/tc); Miriam Doerr (tr); Leung Cho Pan (1/clb); Burlesck (2/clb). **Getty Images:** The Image Bank / Peter Dazeley (tc, cla). **Shutterstock.com:** Seregraff (clb). **42 Dreamstime.com:** Sarkao (br). **Getty Images / iStock:** Andresr (bl). **43 Dreamstime.com:** Ian Allenden (tl); Oksana Byelikova (br). **44 123RF.com:** Erik Lam (bl). **Dreamstime.com:** Willeecole (cla). **44-45 Dreamstime.com:** Alison Gibson. **45 Dreamstime.com:** Sheila Fitzgerald (tr); Onetouchspark (tl); Anna Utekhina (c). **46-47 Dreamstime.com:** Alison Gibson. **46 123RF.com:** Jozef Polc (bc). **47 Alamy Stock Photo:** Imagebroker / Arco / C. Bmke (br); Nature Picture Library / Mark Taylor (cr). **Dreamstime.com:** Isselee (bl); Roman Milert (cl); Pojoslaw (1/cl); Volodymyr Melnyk (c). **48 123RF.com:** tempusfugit (cb). **Dreamstime.com:** Jirk4 (cl); Kadeva (tl); Anton Vierietin (cra). **Getty Images / iStock:** GlobalP (bl). **48-49 Dreamstime.com:** Alison Gibson. **49 Alamy Stock Photo:** Juniors Bildarchiv GmbH / R215 (cl); Tierfotoagentur / S. Schwerdtfeger (tr). **Dreamstime.com:** Dmitry Maslov (cr); Oksun70 (tc); Photodeti (c). **Getty Images / iStock:** E+ / Suzifoo (ca); E+ / dageldog (bc). **Getty Images:** imageBROKER / Arco Christine (tl). **50-51 Dreamstime.com:** Alison Gibson. **50 123RF.com:** Alexandr Ermolaev (tr). **Dreamstime.com:** Shaunda Roberts (ca). **Getty Images:** Photodisc / Martin Leigh (br). **Getty Images / iStock:** skynesher (tl). **51 Dreamstime.com:** Tony Campbell (clb); Sval77 (tl); Rebekah Ramey (cla); Lte100 (cra); Stephanie Zieber (cb); Oksun70 (bl). **Fotolia:** Lipowski (tc). **52-53 Dreamstime.com:** Alison Gibson. **52 Dreamstime.com:** Sergey Lavrentev (bl). **53 Dreamstime.com:** Cristina Villar Martin (cl); Benjamin Simeneta (cr). **55 123RF.com:** Dmytro Momot (cra). **Alamy Stock Photo:** Tierfotoagentur / R. Richter (br). **Dreamstime.com:** Eastmanphoto (cla); Kukotaekaterina (tr); Nataliia Kozynska (crb); Isselee (bl). **56 Dreamstime.com:** Alison Gibson. **57 123RF.com:** Phadungsak Suphorn (1/br). **Dreamstime.com:** Katerina Kovaleva (br); Valentyn75 (cra); Sportmoments (cb). **58 123RF.com:** Daniel Drobik (cla); K. Thalhofer (cl); Andrea Obzerova (1/ca); Anna Goroshnikova (c); Olena Kurashova (br); moskvich1977 (cr). **Dreamstime.com:** Nils Jacobi (bc). **Fotolia:** Eric Isselee (ca). **Getty Images:** DigitalVision / PM Images (cra). **59 Alamy Stock Photo:** Blickwinkel / Klewitz-Seemann (br). **Dreamstime.com:** Elena Vlasova (bc). **Getty Images:** Moment / Randy Riksen Photography (bl). **60 Dreamstime.com:** Christine Bird (bc); Lifeontheside (cra). **61 Alamy Stock Photo:** Juniors Bildarchiv GmbH (ca). **Dreamstime.com:** Yong Hian Lim (crb); Rzoze19 (cb); Svetlana Nezus (b). **62-63 Dreamstime.com:** Alison Gibson. **62 Dreamstime.com:** Elena Kharchenko (br); Barat Roland (tl). **Getty Images:** Stone / Stephen Swintek (bl). **63 Alamy Stock Photo:** ACORN 1 (clb). **64 Dreamstime.com:** Natallia Khlapushyna (cra). **65 Alamy Stock Photo:** SnapTPhotography (br). **Dorling Kindersley:** Peter Anderson / RHS Hampton Court Flower Show 2014 (cr). **Getty Images / iStock:** E+ / northforklight (ca). **Getty Images:** Moment / By Anna Rostova (cla); Moment / A J Withey (cb). **66 Alamy Stock Photo:** Ed Brown Wildlife (cl). **Dreamstime.com:** Andreanita (br); Alison Gibson (t). **Getty Images:** Westend61 (cr). **67 Alamy Stock Photo:** Sergey Uryadnikov (tr). **Dreamstime.com:** Tomonishi (tl). **Getty Images:** Stone / Silvia Otte (crb). **72 Dreamstime.com:** Alison Gibson; Matthijs Kuijpers (tl)

Cover images: *Front:* **Dreamstime.com:** Miroslav Hlavko cra/1, Konstantin Sutyagin crb, Vvoevale cra, Tom Wang cla; **Getty Images:** AndresLopezFotopets / 500px bl; **Getty Images / iStock:** Warmlight br

All other images © Dorling Kindersley